What do you see when you take a look at me?

By Janet Arnold
Illustrated by Jason D. McIntosh

Text copyright © 2020 by Janet Arnold. Illustrations copyright © 2020 by Jason D. McIntosh. All rights reserved. This book or any portion thereof may not be reproduced or used in any manner whatsoever without the express written permission of the publisher except for the use of brief quotations in a book review.

ISBN 978-0-9959758-1-1 | First Printing, 2020 | www.findingsolutions.ca

This book is dedicated to all children.
Believe in yourself and you can do it!

HOW TO USE THIS BOOK:

This book is an introduction to the subject of perseverance and resilience. Children who develop resilience are better equipped to learn from failure and adapt to change. This book allows the reader to connect with the characters' positive traits and enables children to emerge from challenging experiences with a positive sense of themselves and their futures. It helps promote personal strength and the mindset of believing in oneself.

Sample questions to ask while reading this book:

1. What did you think when you first saw the child?
2. What made you think that?
3. How do you think the child felt in the first picture? Why do you think that?
4. How do you think the child is feeling in the second picture? Why do you think that?
5. What challenge or dilemma did the child overcome?
6. What personal strengths did the child possess? What choices did he or she have to make?
7. How are you similar and different from the characters in the book?
8. Tell me about a time that you showed perseverance and resiliency.

What do you see when you take a look at me?

WHAT DO YOU SEE WHEN YOU TAKE A LOOK AT ME?

Do you see someone who feels confident to make new FRIENDS?

what do you see when you take a look at me?

WHAT DO YOU SEE WHEN YOU TAKE A LOOK AT ME?

what do you see when you take a look at me?

WHAT DO YOU SEE WHEN YOU TAKE A LOOK AT ME?

What do you see when you take a look at me?

WHAT DO YOU WANT OTHERS TO **SEE** WHEN THEY TAKE A LOOK AT **YOU?**

Notes for Parents and Educators:

Resilient children may display the following qualities:
- demonstrates an interest in school
- engages in problem-solving
- empathetic toward others
- responsible and trustworthy
- shows initiative
- sets and attains achievable goals
- maintains a sense of purpose and a positive outlook on life
- can act independently
- asks for support when needed

Activities to promote perseverance and resilience:

1. Have children create a "This is me" poster.
   Children can draw, write or cut out various pictures that remind themselves and others of who they are, and goals they want to achieve.

2. Write or draw about a time when you had to cope with a difficult situation. What or who helped you in this situation?

3. Encourage children to interview family members or friends who they admire and have achieved their goals.

ABOUT THE AUTHOR

Janet Arnold is the Mother of two boys. Janet has worked with children and their families for over 23 years. She loves reading books, spending time with her family and creating resources to help others. To learn more about Janet Arnold and her work, visit www.findingsolutions.ca

ABOUT THE ILLUSTRATOR

Jason D. McIntosh is a native to Northern New England and an avid outdoorsman. When he is not writing, designing, or doodling, he can be found adventuring through the woods with his wife and six children or traveling with them through the lands of Middle Earth, Narnia, Redwall Abbey and the like. To see more of his work, visit www.JasonDMcIntosh.com

www.ingramcontent.com/pod-product-compliance
Lightning Source LLC
Chambersburg PA
CBHW041438010526
44118CB00002B/115